TEAM BUILDING FOR MANAGERS

TEAM BUILDING FOR MANAGERS

Series " Management Skills for Managers "
By: D.K. Hawkins
Version 1.1 ~September 2021
Published by D.K. Hawkins at KDP
Copyright ©2021 by D.K. Hawkins. All rights reserved.

No part of this publication may be reproduced, distributed or transmitted in any form or by any means including photocopying, recording or other electronic or mechanical methods or by any information storage or retrieval system without the prior written permission of the publishers, except in the case of very brief quotations embodied in critical reviews and certain other noncommercial uses permitted by copyright law.

All rights reserved, including the right of reproduction in whole or in part in any form.

All information in this book has been carefully researched and checked for factual accuracy. However, the author and publisher make no warranty, express or implied, that the information contained herein is appropriate for every individual, situation, or purpose and assume no responsibility for errors or omissions.

The reader assumes the risk and full responsibility for all actions. The author will not be held responsible for any loss or damage, whether consequential, incidental, special, or otherwise, that may result from the information presented in this book.

All images are free for use or purchased from stock photo sites or royalty-free for commercial use. I have relied on my own observations as well as many different sources for this book, and I have done my best to check facts and give credit where it is due. In the event that any material is used without proper permission, please contact me so that the oversight can be corrected

The information provided in this book is for informational purposes only and is not intended to be a source of advice or credit analysis with respect to the material presented. The information and/or documents contained in this book do not constitute legal or financial advice and should never be used without first consulting with a financial professional to determine what may be best for your individual needs.

The publisher and the author do not make any guarantee or other promise as to any results that may be obtained from using the content of this book. You should never make any investment decision without first consulting with your own financial advisor and conducting your own research and due diligence. To the maximum extent permitted by law, the publisher and the author disclaim any and all liability in the event any information, commentary, analysis, opinions, advice and/or recommendations contained in this book prove to be inaccurate, incomplete or unreliable, or result in any investment or other losses.

Content contained or made available through this book is not intended to and does not constitute legal advice or investment advice and no attorney-client relationship is formed. The publisher and the author are providing this book and its contents on an "as is" basis. Your use of the information in this book is at your own risk.

TABLE OF CONTENTS

TABLE OF CONTENTS 4
INTRODUCTION 6
CHAPTER 1 10
   Team-Building And Its Objectives 10
CHAPTER 2 17
   What Characteristics Define a Winning Team? 17
CHAPTER 3 21
   What Methods Can I Use to Motivate My Team? 21
CHAPTER 4 27
   Involve Everyone in Team-building Activities 27
CHAPTER 5 34
   Team-Building Events And Expectations 34
CHAPTER 6 43
   Increase Competitiveness Through Team-Building Activities
   43
CHAPTER 7 47
   The Fundamentals Of Diversity Management In Team
   Building 47
CHAPTER 8 51
   Open Lines Of Communication To Engage Everyone 51
CHAPTER 9 55
   Successful Team-building Techniques for Managers 55
CHAPTER 10 60

Improve The Effectiveness Of Your Team-Building Strategy..60

CHAPTER 11 66

Using Team-building Games to Rethink Group Strategy 66

CHAPTER 12 70

Team-building Facilitation and Mentoring...........................70

CONCLUSION 76

INTRODUCTION.

Conflict or uncertainty may significantly impair a team's productivity and workflow, and any manager worth their salt will attest to this. Of course, the converse is true. A team that unites gets along, and works will produce high-quality work and a high output volume.

As a manager, you can bring out the best in your team through team-building exercises, both collectively and individually. These can be as complex or simple as you choose, but they will foster a positive team ethic.

The reason you form a team is to achieve success, to work toward a common goal. It makes no difference if the objective is business-related, athletic-related, or something else entirely. It could be a large project or a collection of smaller tasks culminating in a finished product or conclusion. It is irrelevant; what matters is that a productive team can work collaboratively, utterly focused on attaining the goal and achieving success.

By instilling a sense of ownership in each group member for both the project and the result, the team will feel more significant, fostering a shared understanding of responsibility. You can begin by stating your objectives and outlining your strategy for achieving them.

This will foster team commitment, and it is also the ideal moment to discuss any difficulties or reservations your team may have regarding the project. To assist in resolving any future concerns, establish progress indicators - if they are not met, you will know and resolve them; if they are, a sense of accomplishment will radiate throughout the team, encouraging them.

The project on which you are working ultimately dictates the team-building tactics you will employ. It could be a group project in which everyone contributes, a management-led project in which the management has a considerable amount of direction, or the entire organization functioning as one team.

The group-based project will require a greater emphasis on an individual's strengths and abilities because it will require teamwork and independent effort. You will need to promote morale and deal with negative attitudes.

You should strive to incorporate team-building tactics into the project's everyday tasks. While a group-based project will naturally foster a sense of team purpose, by including your tactics, you can ensure that this sense of team purpose is maintained and that each individual retains their voice - and their tasks - while collaborating with their teammates.

Outside of the workplace, it may be worthwhile to devote time to developing your team through team-building events and weekend getaways outside of the workplace. A corporate event management business is an excellent resource for organizing this type of team development exercise, and there are many options available.

Team-building days include different activities that require individuals to collaborate and have proven to be a major success for many businesses.

By merging your ideas into a fun, productive, and exciting setting as a manager, you can help your team work more efficiently. All it requires is little time to examine the objectives you wish to achieve and the skills you want to instill in your team for them to reach their full potential.

Continue reading to learn more.

CHAPTER 1

Team-Building And Its Objectives.

Developing high-performing teams benefits the business, its customers, the teams, and all team members in any organization. To be successful with team-building, it's crucial to maintain a laser-like focus on the objectives and goals and the benefits of team-building for that particular business or workplace.

The Overarching Goals.

Some believe this is about engaging in frivolous games or indulging in costly and pointless extracurricular activities. Managers and business people who believe this will immediately discard the proposal as a complete waste of time and money.

Others who face workplace issues such as group conflict, poor performance, or unmotivated employees may view team-building as a desirable but unrealistic aim. They lack a firm grasp on team development or the critical role of leadership in getting a high performance.

Team development is a PROCESS that occurs over time. The procedure begins with a group of people, two or more, and a leader. The final result of the process is a high-performing team that is highly motivated to improve their performance, has well-developed methods and systems for organizing their workload, and derives enormous satisfaction from their shared accomplishments.

The overall goals are to achieve this level of performance and develop the group through many stages of development until it reaches this level. However, there are distinct processes or phases, each with specific objectives and purposes like with any other process. Concentrating on the RIGHT targets at each step and modifying them as you progress can assist you in achieving high performance.

The Stage One Objectives.

The Forming stage of team formation has very specific aims and purposes. These objectives MUST be met for the group to progress to the next stage. The team leader's responsibility is to guarantee that the goals are met.

The Forming stage's objectives are as follows:

1. To bind the group to learn to know one another and develop a sense of team. Team-building activities will assist in tying them together at this time.

2. To align them with their common purpose, aims, and objectives

3. To build a positive team culture, including shared views, values, and behavioral standards.

4. To define the leader's function

The Second Stage's Objectives.

While some of the initial objectives will be carried forward to this stage, new goals will be created to build the team further. This stage is referred to as the Storming stage, and it is during this stage, members may challenge their shared purpose, leadership, or social standards.

The objectives at this stage are as follows:

1. To keep them focused on their mission and objectives

2. To foster positive working connections among all members by exposing them to different team members.

3. To foster collaborative problem solving and the generation of new ideas.

4. To establish processes that work successfully in conjunction with one another, such as daily huddles,

flash issue solving meetings, regular state of play meetings, and communication systems.

5. To define specific short-term objectives and procedures for commemorating accomplishments and milestones

The Third Stage's Objectives.

After completing the Storming stage, the team will have grown closer and developed a strong feeling of commitment to achieving their shared goal. This is known as the Norming stage, and it occurs when they work effectively together and have good processes and systems in place.

To advance the squad to the next stage, the emphasis shifts.

Only a small percentage of teams reach the fourth level, the high-performing team. Generally, this is because they become trapped in the Norming stage. To propel the team forward, the purpose now is to shift the focus significantly.

To date, the underlying philosophy has been that there is no 'I' in the team. The idea is to bring the team together to accomplish their common goals. The purpose now is to reintroduce the 'I'm into the Team, to keep it together and foster individual greatness and specialization.

At this stage, the objectives are as follows:

1. To develop business expertise, enabling the team and individual members to assume increased responsibility.

2. To foster creativity, innovation, and leadership in the context of specific projects or tasks. The leader delegated authority to the team or smaller project teams.

3. To adapt or change procedures for them to assume increased responsibility. Team meetings are reduced while team project teams are expanded. Rotate leadership of projects or meetings.

4. To encourage the team to establish its objectives.

With this crystallization of team development objectives, you will have a far better chance of efficiently developing your team.

CHAPTER 2

What Characteristics Define a Winning Team?

How do you build a successful team or, in the corporate world, a successful business?

The answer is simple: maintain a good mindset and develop a winning plan! While executives and presidents are responsible for strategy, team builders and managers sustain a positive team spirit.

Positive thinking and team-building are powerful motivators for eliciting the finest performance from employees and keeping them satisfied. Also, team members must believe in both their team or firm and the directive. They must have confidence in their managerial team and their fellow members, keeping in mind that everyone is working toward the same goal.

Team-building Elements.

How do you organize an influential team-building event that contributes to the team's togetherness and performance?

The primary factors are: the event should be enjoyable, even enjoyable (there is no law requiring work to be a miserable, humorless place); the meeting should teach something valuable and communicate the lesson to all team members; workers should be trained how to apply what they learn in their daily routines, and team-building meetings and events should be scheduled regularly. This is the fundamental structure of team-building.

However, there are other alternatives that managers and educators can employ to communicate more effectively with their team members.
Some managers believe that adding a competitive element to events, such as team-building activities, is a practical approach to motivate employees both short and long term.

If this is your objective, you can consider dividing your team into two or smaller teams and having them compete in different sports and activities. This is exceptionally effective at fostering team spirit and motivating employees to complete their assigned tasks.

The Important Role Of Strategy.

A manager or team builder must have a well-defined strategy in mind before organizing the event, throughout the event, and in the aftermath. Effective team planning entails being aware of the meeting's purpose and objectives in advance.

Is there a problem with job performance or with inspiring employees to perform well?

Is there new information that has to be disclosed, or is it more important to develop trust?

All of this should be assessed before the meeting and included in team-building activities. You should structure team activities and the team(s) itself in the most efficient manner possible to accomplish the aim.

Also, communication is essential. You must communicate the same objectives to your employees in a clear and organized manner so that they can recall the meeting's main elements even if they do not recall everything spoken. Instructions on what each team member should do should be explicit and distributed to all team members to ensure no one is left in the dark.

Understanding team-building entails getting to know your teammates on a personal and professional level. A team builder understands that even seemingly insignificant details such as organizing teams or allocating specific persons to other individuals can be a liability or an asset. As a result, team builders must get to know their teammates personally and be familiar with the major archetypes of business personalities.

CHAPTER 3

What Methods Can I Use to Motivate My Team?

This is a frequently asked question when I work with managers. Motivation study is extensive, with every business school, journal, and magazine focusing on it. Theories abound. Motivation, in my experience, is not something that can be "trained" in people. It is not a capability or a skill.

Motivation is an internal process fueled by our inner values and beliefs - those things that are most important to us. When you understand those values and beliefs, you can then determine how to motivate your people.

One option is to infuse your management style with motivating behaviors. Managers that excel at this are not only excellent managers but also excellent leaders.

What does this imply? Here are a few straightforward questions to ponder.

Be a boss your employee's trust and respect - This may sound self-evident, but trust and respect take time to develop and can be lost instantly. Your deeds gain your trust and respect. How dependable are you?

Do you keep your promises?

Do you avoid making unreliable promises?

Are you a defender of your people?

Are you a lone wolf or team player?

Do you acknowledge your team's accomplishments?

Know your team - This refers to your familiarity with your teammates.

What are their preferences and dislikes?

What do they hold dear?

Is there no value?

What latent abilities might they possess that you can recognize and develop?

The most effective managers I've worked with have recognized this.

They have an uncanny ability to grasp what makes their people tick. They take the time to get to know them, whether over a coffee or after work at the pub. They apply their expertise to elicit the finest performance from their people while also addressing their requirements.

Provide your team with exciting and demanding work. Intelligent and ambitious individuals enjoy stimulating work and having a say in what or how things are accomplished.

How often do you carry your employees along in decision-making?

How effective are you at delegating tasks?

Do you delegate or micromanage your work?

Do you assign them projects that will challenge them and aid in their learning?

Do you assist them in their educational endeavors?

Be candid with your feedback - Employees crave input, even difficult feedback.

How often do you give feedback (other than during performance reviews)?

Do you sanitize your messages?

Do you focus on the person's limiting behaviors and reward them?

Are you a coach to your employees?

While providing honest feedback, particularly when there are performance issues, can be challenging, it can be a tremendous motivator when done correctly. A corollary to this is how often do you solicit input from your employees?

Communicate, Communicate - Communication is one of the most effective motivational tools you have, and this is particularly true during times of change. How well do your employees get the big picture - the objectives, the strategy? How well do they comprehend their place within it? How can you assist them in determining their fit?

Don't assume that just because you mentioned something once, the message was received. Individuals perceive information through the "lens" of their values and beliefs. Utilize different channels of communication and, as always, remember that deeds speak louder than words.

Motivating behaviors alone may not ensure a motivated team, and organizational difficulties are sometimes beyond a manager's control. However, focusing on what you can control (and influencing what you can't) may go a long way toward increasing employee motivation, loyalty, and productivity.

Therefore, managers, how do you motivate your teams?! Distribute your wisdom!

CHAPTER 4

Involve Everyone in Team-building Activities.

Team-building activities are an essential component of learning how to lead a team effectively. However, they are more than that. I'm curious how many managers understand that we spend more time with co-workers than with our husbands, wives, children, friends, and other family members.

We generally know very little about our co-workers. Nonetheless, we must negotiate, take direction from, collaborate with, and get along with them daily. Wow.

When most people consider effective team-building activities and how to manage a team, they do so from a manager's perspective. As the manager, they must also see through the employee's eyes. Why?

Because the employee will be responsible for all the tasks assigned by the manager. An employee's behavior has the power to make or ruin a team.

They must understand the value of any team development exercise. Then they must feel they can use the lessons learned. They must believe that the concepts that team-building activities have demonstrated are worth changing their behavior for.

Effective team-building activities and determining how to manage a team begin with the manager determining whether they and those they oversee have the same perspective.

The greatest success will occur when employees feel participated in the process of improving things. The manager's vision, on the other hand, must be shaped and defined. Some inquiries must be made.
Why are we participating in team-building exercises?

What will be different once they have completed their work?

Will we be able to offer suggestions during the process?

Are things going to improve, or will they remain as they are?

And how are we going to maintain things better than they were before?

Responding to these questions is vital to the team's performance following the team-building exercises. Following an effective session (or series of sessions), the manager should manage cooperative individuals.

Issues should be minimized. Every employee should feel more confident about reporting to work each day. (This is the point at which you agree to smile.)

What do team-building activities mean to you as an employee?

Are they significant?

Are they beneficial?

Are they ineffective?

Or do they contribute to making going to work each day a better experience than it was previously? That is important.

The workplace must be an improvement above what it was previously. That is the objective that every manager should strive for. Selecting worthwhile activities of the manager's time away from the office is important if the manager wishes to have a more cohesive team than before the activities.

The varied variety of team-building tools available to managers enables the development of teamwork. The objective is to improve how individuals collaborate continually. At a minimum, the questions posed below should be addressed as part of the planning process for selecting team-building activities.

There are two significant benefits to selecting activities that encourage collaboration. The first is improved job performance, but the most significant is not addressing performance issues monthly.

Team-building exercises are essential in any office setting, even if the team members are geographically dispersed. These activities help to break the ice between co-workers and provide managers with an opportunity to get to know their team members on a more personal level.

The office staff members come from different backgrounds and hence must communicate effectively. As a result, the introduction of team bonding ideas is necessary to break the ice.

The manager's job and responsibility are to include everyone in team bonding activities. Here are some simple strategies for accomplishing this without causing too much disruption:

Include amusement: Any team-building activities that do not end with the team smiling and creating positive memories. A combination of 70% enjoyment and 30% work ensures the activity's success. Also, avoid excessively emphasizing the fun; instead, allow everyone to be themselves and view team bonding ideas as enjoyable.

Your team consists of the following individuals: Recognize the team's profile. In this manner, you'll be aware of their advantages and disadvantages. Attempt to learn about their personal histories and lifestyles. This will assist you in identifying the areas of the team that require attention.

Contact: Team bonding strategies that do not entail a high level of contact and interaction among the members are ineffective. To ensure the exercise's effectiveness, it's important to provide members with a shared platform for communication. Divide the team members into teams composed of an even mix of individuals with varying qualities.

We stated that the activities must be enjoyable, but you must constantly keep the 30% labor component. They will become bored if they cannot connect the activity to something in their work environment.

This helps children understand the value of teamwork. You can connect the activities to games and other activities by mentioning something along the lines of, "This is similar to when the Xyz team completed the following activity and."

The duration of activities is important to consider. It is usually preferable to spread tasks throughout the hour rather than having a single activity drag on for hours. Evenly spaced activities improve your attention span and help maintain the 'fun' component.

Always have backup and alternate activities available if one activity fails to engage participants or you cannot maintain team members' attention.

CHAPTER 5

Team-Building Events And Expectations.

Another catch-all word that we as managers often hear and attempt to respond to is "team-building." Team-building is not a fad. Too often, however, a team-building event is chosen, planned, and implemented without regard for the team-building exercise. A team development exercise or event will not resolve or even address the following:

Low Morale - Using a team-building exercise to combat low morale does not work or resolve the underlying issue. Low employee morale is a symptom of a larger problem inside the department, company, or business. Taking a day off to chat or undertake group activities to unite the group will not resolve the underlying issue.

Tool for Change Management - A team-building exercise is not a tool for change management. While in recent years, as budgets are being squeezed to a breaking point, many leaders have been inclined to conflate the two. It is important that we, as leaders, give these two very distinct tasks the attention they need.

Communication development - Like low morale, communication is an internal issue that cannot be resolved with a yearly shot of team-building.

Team-building events are not the time or place to deliver negative news about the organization or business. Too often, I've witnessed these exercises devolve into a few individuals holding a huge group captive, forcing others to rehash every unpleasant aspect of the work environment.

What is a Team-building Event's Purpose?

The objective of a team-building event is to expose your employees to opportunities to develop new abilities or explore novel ideas and approaches to common problems in a non-threatening atmosphere.

The program is not meant to serve as an extended training session for staff members who already possess or are currently gaining new skills on the job. Nor is it the intention to educate staff and employees on what they "should" be doing to perform their jobs more effectively.

Other than that, the event should provide positive and inspiring alternatives to current behaviors. It should encourage your staff to try new things, think differently, and step outside the "box" to see if they possess a skill set they have never considered applying in their current role within your organization.

Conducting an Assessment of Your Team-building Activities and Expectations.

Unfortunately, team development activities are often thrown together in a moment of desperation. We hire persons not affiliated with our business, product, or service to facilitate activities, plan events, and so forth, "hoping" that the facilitators would supply what the staff needs.

Before selecting a team-building exercise, it is important that you, as the leader, examine the need for the activity and your expectations for the activity. First, you must define what a Team-building Activity is and the expectations you have for the activity.

I've witnessed some outstanding team-building events and have been honored to speak at a few. Therefore, I'd want to spend some time highlighting many of the factors that contributed to these team-building activities being so memorable, well-attended, and well-received by staff, leaders, and visitors.

Planning.

A team-building event requires the same level of preparation and planning as a conference or other sales event. This event should be more than a day spent listening to or participating in the leader's favorite activity or, worse, listening to a speaker unfamiliar with the subject and has not done their homework.

When arranging the event, structured, planned seminars tailored to your team's specific needs should be included. This will depend on the size of your group. The event's organization should be similar to that of a well-run conference or workshop. Dates and sign-up forms should contain all staff members and a spot for comments.

The schedule would look something like this:

In forty-five minutes, we will begin with a welcome and review of the day's activities, followed by introductions of the workshop leaders and facilitators, the locations of significant facilities, and a discussion of optional activities. Please remember that optional activities are that; there should never be any pressure to participate in optional activities.

15-minute intermission.

45 to 60 minutes Workshops I and II.

Workshop I - Inspirational and upbeat - The subject could be dealing with challenging individuals to communication strategies. Still, the keywords here are uplifting and inspirational.

How many workshops have you attended where the subject appeared very relevant based on the title but quickly revealed itself to be a dreary presentation of some "not so interesting" slides that failed to answer any questions or excite you in the slightest?

Workshop II - An hour of skill development with a twist.

How many times have you wondered, as an individual, "How did they do that?" "Man, I wish I knew more about that." We don't have time to "learn" non-traditional talents during our hectic workdays.

This is an excellent opportunity to provide your workers and employees the opportunity to investigate and test a skill set in which they may excel. This is also advantageous for you as a leader, as you are boosting your in-house talent pool.

These courses are held concurrently; by signing up for one or the other, participants commit to learning something new and being positively encouraged to bring their new skills and knowledge back to their workplace. Each session must include a minimum of two seminars to enable your personnel to make growth-enhancing decisions.

Lunch - 60 minutes - is a time for networking. Tables should be set up so that varied groups, not "friends," sit together, and each table should have at least one leader or manager (in listening mode). It's incredible how open people become when they share lunch with strangers, even when a leader or boss is there.

45 to 60 minutes Workshops III and IV.

- Workshops III and IV are structured similarly to the preceding workshops. Although the subject matter is different, it nonetheless contains relevant information that staff will like hearing about.

Closing - The conclusion must be inspirational and ceremonial. Employees who have contributed immensely to the company's success should be honored here. This is the time for you to explain to your employees why they are valuable assets and contribute to their success.

As you can see from the itinerary above, a properly designed team-building event can enable you to spend an entirely productive day and significantly boost your business growth.

When considered as an afterthought, the event does not perform as well. Preparation is essential to the success of any opportunity you create as a leader, whether for your employees or your client base.

Cost.

The cost of a team-building event can range from affordable to prohibitively expensive. Here are a few examples of team-building events that I have facilitated or been a part of. The picnic area of a public park was used, and the concurrent workshops were held beneath park trees.

Due to the low cost of the grounds, my associate hired a barbecue company to cater the event; a realtor friend rented a large empty house to another associate; again, due to the low cost of the day's rental (rental of tables, furniture, etc.), the catering was excellent;

A local museum in our area has two marvelous, unused meeting rooms. Again, a small fee results in a significant impact.

Whether you are operating on a shoestring budget or not, it is essential to remember that your employees are customers just as much as the clients for whom you conduct workshops, seminars, and conferences.

Finally, the cost is small, and the underlying aim of the team-building event is improved through improved effect and employee commitment to future goals.

CHAPTER 6

Increase Competitiveness Through Team-Building Activities.

Competitiveness is important to every organization's success in today's globalized environment. Today's extremely dynamic global market necessitates competitiveness in products and services and, most crucially, teams. Most businesses place a premium on team cohesiveness and engagement while keeping a competitive spirit on the sidelines.

Team competitiveness is dependent on motivation, discipline, and proper support. However, it can be the deciding factor between your team's effectiveness and the rest of the corporate domain.

Team-building experiences and activities provide an excellent opportunity to foster that spirit.

Four strategies for increasing competition during team-building events include the following:

1. Establish the tone.

Before undertaking a team-building activity, establish the tone. While most participants perceive activities as pure enjoyment, they understand that competitiveness plays a significant role in team-building. Selecting a particular definition will assist members in becoming better aligned with the company's goal, vision, and values.

2. Be the first to take the initiative.

Encourage each team to take the initiative during each team-building exercise. You can also award teams that take the initiative; individuals with a killer spirit typically take the initiative in any project, work or assignment.

Once participating teams are compelled to take the initiative, they will naturally develop their bravery. Many team-building exercises are conducted by reputable institutions that design activities that encourage initiative.

3. Establish expectations.

To build a competitive attitude, it is preferable to establish clear expectations. Establishing crystal clear prospects enables teams to focus and concentrate their efforts.

Setting expectations is also a vital component of effective teamwork. This will increase the productivity and competitiveness of your team. This also improves purpose consistency and promotes efficient use of important resources like people, time, and money.

4. Teach steam members how to resolve conflicts.

Excessive competition might increase conflict. It is your sole responsibility to educate them on the most effective methods for resolving internal and external disputes. This is important in the competitive mentality. Through team-building exercises, you may train your team to be polite and manage critiques. Place them in an environment that tests their team spirit.

It is advisable to organize an off-site team-building activity that allows employees to engage and bond. Trekking can be an excellent team-building activity. Allow employees to get together and face a challenge as a team against the backdrop of gorgeous locations.

The four methods outlined above will increase your employees' competitiveness and help your business develop at a rate never seen before.

CHAPTER 7

The Fundamentals Of Diversity Management In Team Building.

At its core, diversity management promotes collaboration among employees. Its mission is to bring men and women from varied backgrounds together and mold them into an effective team focused on a common purpose.

This enables large-scale projects to be performed efficiently and with few complications. Typically, project managers would lead this type of training with team-building ideas, guiding staff through different team-building exercises.

Individuals should first learn how to communicate with one another. One strategy is to divide a large group of individuals into subgroups and ask each member to learn about the backgrounds and personalities of the others. This enables team members to become more acquainted with one another and better understand what individuals have encountered in their own lives.

Also, employees may be required to attend a series of education courses in which preconceptions are deconstructed and debunked. These preconceptions may be based on a person's color, sexual orientation, or age. Often, a psychologist or sociology specialist would be invited in to offer advice and spark conversation. Employees are often urged to participate actively.

Also, group dynamics activities may be included in the session. This can range from doing surveys to replying to inquiries with a raised hand in the air. This can provide insight into people's general attitudes toward specific subjects and aid in developing an overall agreement on some crucial issues.

Managers should establish clearly defined objectives and educate all team members that personal evaluations will be conducted based on these objectives. When success is defined, team members understand what they must do to perform effectively and earn promotions. They should be alright moving ahead if they follow directions and accomplish assigned work.

Occasionally, it is beneficial for team members to gather outside of the office in a low-key area. Whether at a bowling alley, a restaurant, or a sporting event, this can help foster camaraderie and introduce others to one another.

This is especially important when it comes to bringing together employees who would not otherwise interact. Once men and women better understand one another's strengths, all aspects of the project should function more smoothly.

In any event, project managers should ensure that activities are brief and to the point. This should develop a sense of community among all those involved. Also, it should allow them time to do their usual work duties and other chores on schedule.

When brainstorming team-building ideas, managers should consider activities that bring together people of various ethnicities, sexual orientations, ages, religions, and creeds.

By assisting men and women in seeing the good in others, these employees will more readily notice their co-workers' skills and knowledge, which may be utilized to their overall success.

CHAPTER 8

Open Lines Of Communication To Engage Everyone.

The purpose of team-building events and conferences is to get everyone in a company or department to work cooperatively toward a common goal. Communication is an essential aspect of this. Whether via email, phone, or in person, hundreds of encounters occur daily in every office, retail, and warehouse.

Team-building activities attempt to instill the important importance of open communication between all team members. Any communication breakdown might have severe consequences. There are many reasons for a communication breakdown, but three of the most prevalent are listed here.

1. The effect of the silo.

While it may seem self-evident that withholding information can create problems, communication breakdowns are not always deliberate. If a team member is uncomfortable interacting with their teammates or believes their input is unimportant, withholding information might prevent the rest of the team from functioning, and they could.

This could be due to competitiveness, geographical separation, or separate teams that do not want to share with another group. This has been demonstrated often at the team development sessions I facilitate.

There are many causes for the silo effect. Still, it is challenging for the organization to operate at peak efficiency and effectiveness without tearing down walls and fostering collaboration among all teams. Once the teams realize they must work together to tackle the difficulties, the "team-building" portion of the activity is complete.

2. Each individual is significant.

A frequent impediment to communication is a reluctance to communicate candidly with senior management. Participating in team-building activities requiring everyone to work collaboratively to solve riddles or puzzles demonstrates that everyone is an integral team member.

I recall one event in which the teams and judges included everyone involved in the project. From the assembly line workers to the engineers and executives, everyone was on the same team.

It was eye-opening to watch how different levels handled problem-solving. When a group recognizes the importance that each member offers, they might form bonds. When high management recognizes that their company's success is contingent on everyone from management on down, it can influence its morale.

3. Fear of being incorrect.

Some employees may be hesitant to provide opinions that l reflect adversely on them. While not every idea is a good one, employees can learn even if they do not see a direct impact on their contribution.

Managers can learn about the concerns or hurdles that employees experience and the reasons for these issues. Any input demonstrates to a business what its employees are thinking and what they value. Being able to listen to an employee without passing judgment helps establish trust.

Understanding and addressing the issues that employees confront and maintaining open lines of communication go a long way toward focusing everyone on the team's or company's shared purpose.

While communication alone cannot guarantee company success, a lack of it significantly increases failure. Team-building events are an excellent approach to bring the team together and change the current setting.

CHAPTER 9

Successful Team-building Techniques for Managers.

Your team is your business's backbone. How well everything functions together and how you lead it can make or break your company's success. Team-building can be difficult. Each team member offers a unique set of talents and weaknesses to the table.

As the manager and team leader, you also have skills and shortcomings that contribute to your team's success. In today's competitive industry, understanding how to link the puzzle pieces of a successful team is essential. Here are few suggestions to assist you in forming a successful team.

Understand How You Work.

To begin, you must understand how you function.

How would you describe your leadership style?

Are you a good communicator and an effective leader?

Conduct an essential appraisal of yourself, just as you would an employee, and remain receptive to areas for growth. Perhaps you need to improve your communication skills or learn to lead by example. Perhaps sales or leadership training would benefit your management style and assist you in developing a successful team.

Recognize Your Team.

Your team members are more than just a collection of bodies crammed into desk seats. They are individuals with varying personalities, and each contributes a unique component of the team to the group. Make an effort to get to know your teammates. Each week, schedule time for the team to gather, relax and get to know one another.

This sense of camaraderie strengthens relationships between team members and enables the team to function more effectively as a whole. Also, if each team member feels significant and respected, your team will be more effective since everyone feels appreciated and recognizes their thoughts and abilities.

Roles and Responsibilities Are Clearly Defined.

Once you've gotten to know each team member and identified their strengths and limitations, you may define each team member's duties and responsibilities. Perhaps one team member is not particularly skilled at their profession but excels at keeping the team on target.

This individual will contribute significantly to the team's success by keeping the team moving and saving you money by avoiding poor judgments or allowing the team to stagnate.

Another team member may possess exceptional communication skills and the ability to relate to a wide variety of people. This individual is valuable because they can define the team's objectives and effectively communicate them to its members.

Your team is similar to a puzzle made up of many unique components. You must understand how they all fit together and the roles they each perform on the squad. You may then capitalize on their strengths and abilities and clearly define their roles within the team to ensure that it functions properly.

Recognize that feedback is a two-way street.

Feedback is a priceless resource. It informs you of your team's performance and places for improvement. You can have a formal or informal feedback system. By being proactive with feedback, you may assist your staff in improving each day and avoiding severe difficulties. Avoid being a reactive manager; instead, be proactive by listening to your team's input and providing constructive feedback of your own.

Recognize, Respect, and Commend.

Everybody enjoys being rewarded, and everyone values respect. Recognize and respect a team member who goes above and beyond. This demonstrates your team's worth, and they will exert increased effort toward their goal. Take time to enjoy your accomplishments.

Even minor accomplishments deserve recognition, even as simple as having box lunches provided one day. Positive reinforcement and recognition will assist in motivating and retaining your team's commitment to working well together.

As a team leader and manager, you are responsible for developing an effective team and keeping them on track. Utilize these five techniques to form a successful team and complete the task at hand.

When you know your team's strengths and limitations, you can collaborate to establish an effective and successful team that will not only meet but surpass your company's goals.

CHAPTER 10

Improve The Effectiveness Of Your Team-Building Strategy.

Yes, it is important to work on your team dynamics daily, monitoring and modifying as necessary. However, particularly developed team-building days have their place. Just remember that if you're going to host a team-building event, it must provide value. After all, training is costly, and even participants expect a return on their time and effort.

It is irrelevant if you engage in team-building activities, compile a list of team rules or discuss team issues. What matters most is how you do something, not what you do. Understanding what teams require to function well will enable you to understand better how to improve team procedures (not just during a specific team-building event but also on a day-to-day basis).

What Teams Require.

To be productive - to function as a cohesive unit and accomplish more than is feasible individually - teams require some important aspects in their surroundings. While achieving these characteristics is not difficult, they do need some work on the side of the team leader or business owner.

These elements have been demonstrated repeatedly in research to be essential for effective teams. They are not "new age," "touchy-feely," or "time-wasters." They are the fundamentals of teamwork, and firms that realize their value and seek to sustain them are rewarded with teams that outperform their more ordinary counterparts by a wide margin.

Strengthening Team Performance.

If you intend to boost your team's performance, it's not only about "whipping them into shape." It's about establishing the optimal setting for them to perform at their peak.

It's also about accepting and understanding your job as a leader/coach and developing the abilities necessary to build the team you deserve. As the world's finest sporting coaches often state, the coach's career is jeopardized when a team fails to perform!

Therefore, let us examine what a team requires to be effective.

The Five Areas of Effectiveness.

1. Mission of the Team. Every member of the team should understand why the team performs what it does. What is the business attempting to accomplish, and how does the team contribute to this effort?

Every team member must understand the team's priorities, particularly when they change and how working to the wrong priorities impairs the team's ability to execute its purpose.

2. Goal Accomplishment. The team leader's role is to assist the team in defining their objectives (both collective and individual) and provide feedback on their progress toward achieving these objectives. This must be constant, truthful, and non-blaming.

The team, both collectively and individually, must also contribute to the development of these aims. Above all, the team leader must assist the team in achieving its objectives by offering assistance and resources.

3. Self-determination. While the team must work toward attaining company objectives and according to corporate norms, the team and its members require some degree of autonomy in decision-making and activity.

That doesn't mean anything goes. Still, it does imply that we all have a voice in our daily lives, including our professional life, rather than imposing authority; attempt to develop a team's skill level through guidance.

Both technical and interpersonal abilities (together referred to as Emotional Intelligence) are necessary for team members to assume ownership of their jobs and act appropriately.

Guidance and role modeling will foster ownership and independence, allowing the team leader to "delegate" many operational chores and focus on more important management responsibilities.

4. Transparent, forthright communication. Communication must be candid, timely, and two-way. This is not a master-slave relationship but rather an engagement between adults on an equal footing (of course, this takes a high level of emotional intelligence from both parties).

When workers are treated with dignity and respect, the vast majority respond with increased effort and outcomes. When everyone feels comfortable courteously expressing themselves, the entire team performs better and the consumer notices! Conflict is minimized and addressed more quickly, and individuals have a better handle on their behaviors.

5. Positive role models and social standards. Individuals learn best through observation, analysis, and practice.

What are they observing in your business when they observe the Team Leader's behavior?

Are the Team Leader and all other supervisors demonstrating the type of behavior they want their team members to exhibit?
Or is it more of a "do as I say, not as I do" situation?

Team members must have positive role models, and time and effort must be invested in training and skill development to extract the maximum performance from each team member.

Finally, team-building is a necessary component of your entire business improvement plan. Do not use it as a band-aid or a panacea; it is ineffective in both cases. It must flow naturally from the various everyday actions you perform to maintain your team healthy.

CHAPTER 11

Using Team-building Games to Rethink Group Strategy.

Focusing on group methods and emphasizing various strengths and shortcomings through team-building activities can significantly increase any group or organization's productivity.

Using fundamental psychological principles and established values, dedicated change management instructors may assist any team in achieving greater success in their work environment.

Stimulating and enjoyable activities indoors or outdoors in different locations across the country can be an excellent method for any company to set new priorities and adaptable techniques.

Teammates can gain a new perspective on the workplace and benefit from new techniques and thinking. Utilizing a fully authorized team-building course can make all the difference in providing a required boost to a company team.

The Positive Consequences of Problem Solving.

Each company and employee confronts everyday obstacles and issues that must be addressed and resolved. The gap between successful and failed organizations is often determined by their ability to solve these difficulties.

This is just one area in which corporate team-building games can be beneficial. Group strengthening activities can help raise morale and improve communication for individuals and group members based on fundamental psychological concepts.

Fully accredited team development instructors may foster team development differently by removing individuals from their everyday work contexts to focus on vital skills. A working break at one of the country's many locales might prove to be a significant and rewarding investment for any business or enterprise.

How Team-building Games Can Help You Feel More Satisfied With Your Job.

Every manager and team leader should be concerned with increasing employee and colleague job satisfaction and morale. Many studies have decisively demonstrated that contented employees are more productive and ultimately more beneficial to their employers than disgruntled employees.

Therefore, it should be the objective of every prudent manager to employ any strategy that improves these important perceptions of value and worth. A fully approved group strategy course is one of the most effective ways to accomplish this.

Qualified instructors can collaborate with team leaders and managers to create a program tailored to each group of colleagues and co-workers' unique needs. Indoor and outdoor team-building activities can make a significant difference in terms of enhancing workplace relationships and communication.

Businesses and organizations of all types can significantly benefit from such work breaks and would be well to investigate the potential benefits.

CHAPTER 12

Team-building Facilitation and Mentoring.

Do mentors play a role in team development? They appear to do so, and it also stands to reason that when a strong team member mentors a newcomer or a weaker team member, the outcomes are astounding. It's exciting to see what that younger or newer team member is capable of accomplishing.

As a manager, it is important to facilitate this form of mentorship among select team members when managing them. If the team has three or four solid players, each of them should buddy one or two of the squad's junior members. Attempting to establish common bonds will assist in this process.

There are various ways to accomplish this, and with the proper facilitation, it can become as natural as riding a bicycle. All too often, junior team members are aware that they cannot compete at the same level as senior team members who possess the necessary credentials and experience to play.

However, this doesn't imply that they will not do so in the future; it is essential to pair them with a superstar with the proper mentality to ensure their success.

Not every great player possesses the personality attributes or the patience to serve as a father figure to members of the junior squad. Many lack the ability, and they can do more harm than good to a younger team member.

When managing a team, it's important to identify which employees can assist others and bring the rest of the team up. Nonetheless, some personality types are capable of filling this job. I hope you will consider this.

Promotion is always a significant event. The most challenging part is constantly stepping up and not hiding behind what you used to accomplish at your previous work. The transition from Manager to Executive is one of the most significant.

Executives must consider and act on issues that are quite distinct from those faced by their management counterparts. The simplest way to summarize is that we must think and manage strategically, which is not something that most people are accustomed to.

There is another issue as well. Executive teams are typically comprised of similarly motivated and driven individuals. Any team with too many similarities and not enough variances risks becoming unbalanced to the point of dysfunction and falling victim to "groupthink," in which team members agree on everything, even when their decisions are radically incorrect. Executive team-building may be beneficial.

Undoubtedly, one of the commonalities will be that all team members will be intelligent enough to overcome the team's weaknesses if they grasp them in the first place. Thus, if a well-chosen team activity assists them in identifying the issue, the team can begin to mend itself.

To summarize, if an executive team chooses a team-building option, it should focus on strategic management. During the brief, it will identify team shortcomings and initiate putting in place measures to avoid them.

When it comes to operating strategically, the first issue that any new Executive has is defining a strategy. Not what "their" plan is but how one looks in practice. A process is a hybrid of a vision, a goal, and a methodology. It is the destination an organization desires to reach, the time frame it wishes to be there, and the approach it wishes to follow along the way.

Strategic management is about implementing the plan consistently throughout the organization to make it helpful and ultimately effective. Each employee must comprehend what it means for their job and use it when making day-to-day decisions, and strategic management is all about bringing that vision to fruition.

Generally, team-building activities are not designed to draw attention to strategic issues. Tactical decision-making is typically the order of the day. Those adept at "shooting from the hip" fare better than those who prefer to plan meticulously before beginning.

Thus, the activity chosen must bear this in mind. The exercise must be comprehensive and lengthy enough to provide strategic thinkers a genuine chance to influence the team's approach. It should also allow teams to employ that strategy throughout the activity so that the success or failure of the team's approach can be evaluated during debriefing.

When it comes to debriefing, that session is the most important component of the entire exercise. The strategy must be properly thought out and primarily conducted by the team itself to truly identify the team's flaws. That is, it must be documented.

A facilitator's function at this point should be to assist the team in identifying the challenges created by their approach to the task, not to stand in front and tell them where they went wrong. That rarely assists a team in comprehending the available learning or transferring it to the workplace, where it can make a difference.

When planning a team away day for executive-level managers, remember that you must offer them something appropriate for their type of team and task. That is an excellent strategy!

CONCLUSION

"None of us is as smart as all of us," is a famous saying by Ken Blanchard. Although some may question if it is grammatically correct, the meaning of the quote is quite true. A united effort is always more productive than an individual effort. By concentrating on each individual's skills, a good team may accomplish even more.

The fundamental ingredient to an efficient team is the team members. There have been countless times where group projects fail or function less smoothly than they should due to one individual not pulling their weight.

Eric Fox suggested the primary tasks of a workgroup are as follows: advancer (idea communicator), creator (idea generator), the executor (idea implementer) refiner (idea challenger), and flexible worker for all other jobs. It is crucial to have each group member in a role they are most naturally comfortable in. This might be due to a lack of laziness, motivation or the member may not comprehend their aims for the group.

I have been in very effective and less effective groups. As a manager with experience, I have been a member of a particular team where many co-workers I just bonded with could have the clients in and out in no time. I suppose this was because we could communicate the same way and had similar cognitive patterns.

Because we all had the same understanding, there was less explanation, and more work finished. As a manager, I often consider what I can do in a group setting and what my actions enable others to accomplish with my cognitive style.

However, I may neglect the idea that others may not share my perspective and choose to do something else. That is why it is essential to convey the objectives to all stakeholders effectively. Thanks for Reading

Management Skills for Managers

1. Time Management for Managers
2. Employee Coaching for Managers
3. Team Building for Managers
4. Self Confidence for Managers
5. Negotiation Skills for Managers
6. Customer Service Skills for Managers
7. Coming soon

www.ingramcontent.com/pod-product-compliance
Lightning Source LLC
Chambersburg PA
CBHW070121230526
45472CB00004B/1361